GOD'S IDEAL
WOMAN

GOD'S IDEAL WOMAN

By
Clifford Lewis

Foreword by
MRS. WILLIAM A. (BILLY) SUNDAY

A Commendation by
MRS. JOHN R. RICE

Post Office Box 1099 • Murfreesboro, Tennessee 37133

INTRODUCTION

"If I had heard that message twenty years ago, I am sure I would not have made that awful mistake that I made, and my broken heart and home could have been prevented," said a sad-faced woman as she met me in the aisle of a church after a service for women and girls only. Another mother said, "Those words of warning should be in print. I am so thankful that my daughters heard you this afternoon. Every woman and girl in America and other lands needs the message that you have just given."

After hearing such encouraging remarks for several years in all sections of America, Canada and abroad, I felt definitely lead to write out the messages from only a few notes. I am happy that the testimony of this book will reach into many places where I can never go personally.

Let me express my appreciation to those who are indicating their desire to help spread these messages throughout the country. Orders are constantly coming in even before the book is printed. Some are ordering several copies to use as gifts for various occasions. How I wish that there was some way to get a copy of this book into every home in America and that a large number could be sent to other countries. Will you pass your book around so that your relatives, friends and neighbors may read it?

Every word of every sentence has been bathed in earnest prayer. Every copy will be sent forth with a prayer behind it. We are praying that as a result of reading its pages, the unsaved may be pointed to the

Lord Jesus Christ; the defeated, backslidden Christians may return to fellowship and constant victory; and the saints of God may be fired with a new zeal to be soul winners. We are also praying that the frivolous may heed the words of warning, the discouraged may be comforted, the lonely ones may be cheered, and thousands of homes will be made happier and more harmonious because of the establishment, or reestablishment, of family altars. By faith we are claiming victory for many hearts and homes, and we are thanking our Father in advance for what He is going to do.

Mrs. Lewis and I are constantly traveling up and down the land trying to get the Gospel to as many people as possible. We need and will be deeply grateful for your daily prayers. If there is any service that we can render at any time, please feel free to write us. We are always glad to receive the prayer requests and testimonies of those who read our books.

CLIFFORD LEWIS

(Publisher's Note: Dr. Lewis went to be with the Lord November 19, 1985.)

FOREWORD

Encouragement and the knowledge of the true way out for our youth is needed as never before in our blessed land. I thank God and take courage that scores and even hundreds, such as Clifford Lewis represents, are espousing the cause of Christianity and are determined to try and win our young folks. Knowing it to be the only really worthwhile program for the world today, I am glad they are concentrating on and appealing to the youth of our nation. More power to you, Clifford!

We need words of warning and signposts to find our way out of the dense fog that surrounds us, and I pray and trust that this book, *God's Ideal Woman,* will be read and that the light will break in on the lives and hearts of tens of thousands who will find our Lord as their Saviour. Then they will go out and testify and become witnesses to the saving and keeping power of Jesus our Lord.

Mrs. W. A. (Billy) Sunday

Clifford Lewis

A COMMENDATION

I keep this book on my bedside table to read and refer to often. In it the teenage girl and the mature woman will find the answer to the questions and problems that baffle women of every age.

First, it sets out to help the teenage girl to wisely and discreetly set the course for her life; how to avoid the pitfalls and temptations common to a young girl; how to choose worthy ambitions, select the right friends, and set a high standard of conduct for her own life.

The second chapter is addressed to the woman who will not marry; how she should be self-supporting and happy in God's appointment, surrendering her life to Him.

Every girl should familiarize herself with the lessons on love, dating and marriage as set forth in chapter 3. Dr. Lewis emphasizes five "don'ts" and five "do's" in selecting a husband.

How to have a happy, succcessful Christian home is portrayed in chapter 4. There are some twenty Bible passages to show exactly how.

Chapter 5 deals with the responsibility of motherhood and its rewards.

Chapter 6 closes the book with the challenge of Proverbs 31, God's concise description of the virtuous woman; how she is chaste, energetic, physically fit, economical, unselfish, prepared, honorable, prudent, lovable, God-fearing and rewarded.

The way of salvation is also clearly presented. I trust the book will be widely distributed and a blessing to many.

Mrs. John R. Rice

CONTENTS

CHAPTER I

DON'T BE A SILLY GIRL!

A silly girl can be frivolous, selfish, thoughtless, ungrateful, proud, intemperate, impure, unkind, disrespectful, stubborn, tactless, willful, disobedient, untrustworthy, without worthy ambitions, careless about her friends, and devoid of high standards. Some of these characteristics are discussed in other chapters in this book, but let us notice the last three mentioned above.

WITHOUT WORTHY AMBITIONS

"What are you living for?" someone asked a young girl. "For the kick I can get out of life," she quickly replied. Only a silly girl would make such a statement, and yet we should be very sympathetic with such young people.

The majority of girls are so afraid that someone will think of them as "wallflowers," "flat tires," "old fogies" and "tied to mama's apron strings," that they make the silly mistake of adopting the selfish, stubborn philosophy expressed in such terms as "be a good sport"; "follow the gang"; "hit the pace"; "keep up with the age"; "roll 'em high"; "the sky is the limit"; and "not young but once, so have a big time."

Girls, remember this! It is the devil's lie that you must sow your wild oats and go over "Fool's Hill." Many are wrecked before they get over the hill; and don't forget the sad fact that if you sow wild oats, you must sooner or later reap a wild harvest.

"Be not deceived; God is not mocked: for whatsoever a man soweth, that shall he also reap. For he that soweth to his flesh shall of the flesh reap corruption; but he that soweth to the Spirit shall of the Spirit reap life everlasting."—Gal. 6:7, 8.

"For they have sown the wind, and they shall reap the whirlwind."—Hos. 8:7.

"Even as I have seen, they that plow iniquity, and sow wickedness, reap the same."—Job 4:8.

Every girl should be ambitious to start sowing good seed early in life. She should be ambitious to live pure, unselfish, humble, temperate and obedient. Worthy ambition prompts her to be thoughtful, kind, trustworthy, tactful, respectful and grateful.

The only way to possess worthy ambitions is to know the Lord Jesus Christ as your personal Saviour and love Him with all your heart. As a Christian, your greatest desire and ambition is to do His precious will and to win lost souls from darkness to light.

CARELESS ABOUT HER FRIENDS

You cannot be too careful about your friends. They will help to make you or break you. We are prone to become like those with whom we associate. Here is a statement worth remembering: When you leave out one letter, the word *friend* is changed to *fiend*. That "r" should stand for reality.

It is possible to let your heart run away with your head. It is easy to make a mistake in the choice of friends. Be sure that they are real. Are you better or worse after being with them? Someone has said that a real friend is one who sees the best that is in you, appeals to that best, and will help you to work out the best for your life. We know that a true friend will also see our mistakes and will help us to overcome them.

I warn you to be careful about getting a crush on anyone. A crush oftentimes has a detrimental reaction on the mind and body of a person. It is dangerous to get a crush on a member of either sex. Friendship should be thought of as a very sacred thing. If it is real, it will be built on a firm foundation and not a "crushy" one.

Don't get chummy with the wrong people. You do not realize the evil you permit to enter your life when you keep company with folk who are impure in thought, word or deed. The tragic story of many who have fallen is: "I started going with the wrong person or crowd." You should sever relationships at once with anyone who is pulling you toward the world. Why should you throw yourself away to one like that?

The friendship of Jonathan, the prince, and David, the shepherd boy, is expressed in the verse, "The Lord be between me and thee" (I Sam. 20:42). If Christ is between you and your friend, you are always drawn closer to each other as you are drawn closer to Him. Friends should love each other for Christ's sake.

DEVOID OF HIGH STANDARDS

The silly girl has no high standards for life. Many girls are deceived by thinking that in order to be popular with the opposite sex, she must be vulgar in her speech, daring in her dress and loose in her ways. She believes that if she rides the waves of modern society, she must go in for garish cosmetics, cigarettes, cocktails and wild parties. You may attract a "beast" or "human hawk" by those methods, but you will never attract a decent man.

Girls should be very careful about habits. The average girl has no idea of the physical effect of smoking and drinking. These habits soon wreck your will power and your nerves. The thing that started as a so-called pleasure ends in slavery. I have heard them desperately say, "Oh, if I could only quit these things!"

Thousands of girls start the downward path every year through the modern dance. Someone described the dance as a "hugging match set to music." The quickest way to kill the dance is to take sex out of it. The devil uses the immodest bodily contact of the dance to excite wicked passions which wreck multitudes of youth. Unholy desires result from dancing; so the only safe thing to do is to abstain completely. Do you have enough backbone to say, "No!"?

Many people try to justify dancing at home and school. These places feed the public dance halls. You don't have to take dancing just because it is taught in many of our public schools. Stand alone if necessary! Don't follow the crowd! The majority of young people only have a cotton string with ribs dangling from it for a backbone. They remind me of a jellyfish. The wind of popularity blows them this way, that way, and the other way. Are you in this class?

Influence certainly should be considered in this discussion. At the close of a service, a young lady came forward under deep conviction. She said, "I am worried about my influence. I taught my boyfriend to dance after his mother begged me not to do it. Since then I have become a Christian and have stopped dancing, but I can't get him to stop. His dancing leads him to do other sinful things. He is breaking his mother's heart, and I feel that I am responsible for it all."

Millions of our youth are taught evil by the suggestive things they see in the movies. The movie theaters are being used to poison the minds of children and to fill the jails with youthful criminals. I understand that the following blasphemous statement appeared some time ago in a movie magazine: "Vice pays on the screen; virtue will not make expenses." The majority of the outstanding actors and actresses have been divorced more than once.

During the last few years a great many people, young and old, have felt convicted and have stopped attending the movies. They feel that they cannot waste their money or influence on an institution that is doing so much harm.

The following poem has a real challenge:

When you think or speak or read or write;
When you sing or walk or seek for delight;
To be kept from all wrong when at home or abroad,
Live always as under the eyes of the Lord.

Whatever you think, never think what you feel
You would blush in the presence of God to reveal.
Whatever you speak in a whisper or clear,
Say nothing you would not like Jesus to hear.

Whatever you read, though the page may allure,
Read nothing unless you are perfectly sure
Consternation would not be seen in your look,
If God should say solemnly, "Show Me that book!"

Whatever you write, though in haste or in heed,
Write nothing you would not like Jesus to read.
Whatever you sing, in the midst of your glees,
Sing nothing His listening ear would displease.

Wherever you go, never go where you'd fear
God's question being asked, "What doest thou here?"
Turn away from pleasures you'd shrink from pursuing,
If God should look down and say, "What are you doing?"

If you desire to know what is right and wrong, I suggest that you go to the Bible for your standards. People may give you wrong advice about certain things, but God's Word is always right. The first thing to be sure about is that you are saved. Then be sure that you are living a surrendered life. Are these two facts glorious realities in your life? If so, you will not be bothered with that common question, "What is the harm?" Can you pray about everything that you do and ask God's blessing upon it? Are you willing to be honest so you can see the truth as revealed in the Bible? Please study prayerfully the following verses:

"And whatsoever ye do in word or deed, do all in the name of the Lord Jesus, giving thanks to God and the Father by him."—Col. 3:17.

"Whether therefore ye eat, or drink, or whatsoever ye do,

do all to the glory of God."—I Cor. 10:31.

"Let your light so shine before men, that they may see your good works, and glorify your Father which is in heaven."— Matt. 5:16.

"It is good neither to eat flesh, nor to drink wine, nor anything whereby thy brother stumbleth, or is offended, or is made weak."—Rom. 14:21.

"For if ye live after the flesh, ye shall die: but if ye through the Spirit do mortify the deeds of the body, ye shall live. For as many as are led by the Spirit of God, they are the sons of God."—Rom. 8:13, 14.

"I beseech you therefore, brethren, by the mercies of God, that you present your bodies a living sacrifice, holy, acceptable unto God, which is your reasonable service. And be not conformed to this world: but be ye transformed by the renewing of your mind, that ye may prove what is that good, and acceptable, and perfect will of God."—Rom. 12:1, 2.

"And if thy right eye offend thee, pluck it out, and cast it from thee: for it is profitable for thee that one of thy members should perish, and not that thy whole body should be cast into hell. And if thy right hand offend thee, cut it off, and cast it from thee: for it is profitable for thee that one of thy members should perish, and not that thy whole body should be cast into hell."—Matt. 5:29, 30.

"Enter ye in at the strait gate: for wide is the gate, and broad is the way, that leadeth to destruction, and many there be which go in thereat: Because strait is the gate, and narrow is the way, which leadeth unto life, and few there

be that find it."—Matt. 7:13, 14.

"Nevertheless the foundation of God standeth sure, having this seal, The Lord knoweth them that are his. And, Let every one that nameth the name of Christ depart from iniquity."—II Tim. 2:19.

"Abstain from all appearance of evil."—I Thess. 5:22.

"Love not the world, neither the things that are in the world. If any man love the world, the love of the Father is not in him."—I John 2:15.

"Therefore if any man be in Christ, he is a new creature: old things are passed away; behold, all things are become new."—II Cor. 5:17.

"Wherefore come out from among them, and be ye separate, saith the Lord, and touch not the unclean thing; and I will receive you."—II Cor. 6:17.

"I am crucified with Christ: nevertheless I live; yet not I, but Christ liveth in me: and the life which I now live in the flesh I live by the faith of the Son of God, who loved me, and gave himself for me."—Gal. 2:20.

"Wherefore seeing we also are compassed about with so great a cloud of witnesses, let us lay aside every weight, and the sin which doth so easily beset us, and let us run with patience the race that is set before us, Looking unto Jesus the author and finisher of our faith; who for the joy that was set before him endured the cross, despising the shame, and is set down at the right hand of the throne of God."—Heb. 12:1, 2.

"If ye then be risen with Christ, seek those things which

*are above, where Christ sitteth on the right hand of God.
Set your affection on things above, not on things on the
earth. For ye are dead, and your life is hid with Christ in
God."*—Col. 3:1–3.

MY HEART'S DESIRE

Cleanse my heart and fill me with Thy Spirit;
Satisfy the longings of my soul.
I crown Thee King and bid Thee hold the scepter;
Yielding all, I'm now 'neath Thy control.
Have Thy way, for Thee alone I'll follow;
Too long I've followed self, rejecting Thee.
Now I lay my ALL upon the altar;
Sanctify the gift and dwell with me.

All my plans and all of my ambitions,
All my dreams and all my earthly store,
Friends with all their ties that closely bind me,
I ask Thee Lord to hold forevermore.
Crucify the self that ruled within me;
I'll take the cross and gladly follow Thee.
Stamp Thy likeness on my heart forever
Until Thy blessed image all shall see.

Stir my heart with love's intensest ardor;
Teach me how to give, to serve, to pray;
Make my heart and life an unchoked channel
Of blessing to my fellowmen each day.
Keep me humble, lowly and submissive,
Sweet in spirit, kind in thought and deed,
Until all who look see Jesus only;
And precious souls to Thee, I then may lead!
—Helen G. Riggs

Chapter II

ADVICE TO THE SINGLE WOMAN

One thing worse than being a single woman is getting the wrong man for a husband. It is far better to be a bachelorette or "unclaimed blessing," than to have your heart crushed and home broken by an unfortunate marriage. There are plenty of women who "wish they were single again."

Are you fighting life's battle alone while your heart yearns for a loving mate, a happy home, and little ones to care for? Are you lonely, envious, and even discouraged because some of your best friends are happily married and you seem to be left behind? Do you consider unmarried life a big problem, and is it hard to face this thing which seems to be the inevitable?

I trust that this explanation will be comforting to you. A little girl whispered to me once, "My aunt certainly likes you because you say such comforting things about single women, and she's one of 'em." I realize that I am discussing a very delicate subject, and I am praying for wisdom as I continue writing this chapter. I humbly suggest three things:

BE SELF-SUPPORTING

Every girl should make the proper preparation to be self-supporting. The majority of girls can get a good education if they have sufficient determination. It is nice to have the ability to "paddle your own canoe." You can be happy in your work. There are plenty of activities to give scope to your gifts and an outlet for your womanhood. No girl need become a "sour old maid" or the pathetic victim of self-pity. Don't ever be foolish enough to think that you are unwanted, useless or overlooked.

If you are in the valley of sorrow, get out at once! I remember an interesting and helpful motto that I saw in the home of a friend in England. "Today is the tomorrow that you worried about yesterday, and all is well." Cultivate the art of making and keeping friends; have some good hobbies and interest others in them; stay busy in worthwhile activities; plan your vacations so that you can take some nice trips to different parts of the country, and abroad, if possible; and spend plenty of time reading good literature.

Many girls seem to have no real ambition in life. Some are resting on their oars of past accomplishments. It should be encouraging to know that you can do everything that you are supposed to do. "I can do all things through Christ which strengtheneth me" (Phil. 4:13).

It isn't so much the thing you've done
  That should occupy your mind;
 It is better far to look ahead
  Than it is to look behind.
Let others praise your accomplished work,
  If they will; but as for you,
It isn't so much the thing you've done
  As the thing you are going to do.

When you've finished a task, don't think it is time
  To take an unlimited rest;
Just think of the work that is coming next
  And how you can do it best.
A finished job, if its been well done,
  Is a pleasant thing to view;
But always the most important thing
  Is the thing you are going to do.

So look ahead and make your plans
  For whatever may come to hand;
Then start with a will to do the job,
  And do it as you have planned.
You've a right to be proud of the thing you have done,
  If it's done well, that is true;
But the thing on which you should keep your mind
  Is the thing you are going to do.

Don't neglect your prayer life and your daily Bible reading. Have you ever read the Bible all the way through? You will find within the lids of the Bible a solution for every problem in your life. It is a very practical book. The central theme of the Bible is the Lord Jesus Christ. He wants to help you in all your work. He will change your job into a position. You should think of your work not as secular, but as sacred. When temptations come, Christ will give you power to overcome; when sorrow comes, He is near to comfort and cheer; when misunderstanding comes, He is ever present and always understands. Others may fail you, but Christ will never let you down. "God is our refuge and strength, a very present help in trouble" (Ps. 46:1). "As one whom his mother comforteth, so will I comfort you" (Isa. 66:13). "Like as a father pitieth his children, so the Lord pitieth them that fear him" (Ps. 103:13). "No good thing will he withhold from them that walk uprightly" (Ps. 84:11). "Nay, in all these things we are more than conquerors through him that loved us" (Rom. 8:37).

> He's helping me now—this moment,
> Though I may not see it or hear,
> Perhaps by a friend far distant,
> Perhaps by a stranger near,
> Perhaps by a spoken message,
> Perhaps by the printed word;
> In ways that I know and know not,
> I have the help of the Lord.
>
> He's keeping me now—this moment,
> However I need it most,
> Perhaps by a single angel,
> Perhaps by a mighty host,
> Perhaps by the chain that frets me
> Or the walls that shut me in;
> In ways that I know and know not,
> He keeps me from harm or sin.
>
> He's guiding me now—this moment,
> In the pathways easy or hard,
> Perhaps by a door wide open,
> Perhaps by a door fast barred,
> Perhaps by a joy withholden,
> Perhaps by a gladness given;
> In ways that I know and know not,
> He's leading me up to Heaven.

He's using me now—this moment,
And whether I go or stand,
Perhaps by a plan accomplished,
Perhaps when He stays my hand,
Perhaps by a word in season,
Perhaps by a silent prayer;
In ways that I know and know not,
His labor of love I share.
—ANNIE JOHNSON FLINT
Copyright by Evangelical Publishers, Toronto, Canada

DESIRE GOD'S WILL

I understand that boy babies die more easily than girls; therefore, the population is uneven. It seems that there are more Christian girls than Christian boys; so things are uneven again. We naturally draw the conclusion that it is not God's will for every girl to be married. We read in II Cor. 6:14,

"Be ye not unequally yoked together with unbelievers: for what fellowship hath righteousness with unrighteousness? and what communion hath light with darkness?"

There is nothing better than being married if you are sure you are in the will of God. There is nothing more tragic than to marry out of God's will. Here is a story told me by a woman who attended one of our campaigns:

"I was converted when I was quite young. I later felt a definite call to the foreign mission field. I was selfish and stubborn and refused the call of God. I wanted a home and family, and now I have both; but I don't have that deep peace in my heart that comes only by doing God's will. I am working in the church, trying to give my second best, but I regret that I did not give Him my first best."

Are you willing to say good-bye to your selfish plans and to follow Christ by faith from day to day?

> If we could see beyond today
> As God can see;
> If all the clouds should roll away,
> The shadows flee;
> O'er present griefs we would not fret;
> Each sorrow we would soon forget,
> For many joys are waiting yet
> For you and me.

> If we could know beyond today
> As God doth know,
> Why dearest treasures pass away
> And tears must flow;
> And why the darkness leads to light;
> Why dreary paths will soon grow bright;
> Some day life's wrongs will be made right—
> Faith tells me so.

> "If we could see, if we could know,"
> We often say;
> But God in love a veil doth throw
> Across our way.
> We cannot see what lies before,
> And so we cling to Him the more;
> He leads us till this life is o'er;
> Trust and obey.

GIVE CHRIST YOUR ALL

On my trip around the world I found that some of the most successful missionaries were unmarried ladies. Some of them could have been married too, but God had a job for them to do alone. Florence Nightingale, Frances Willard, Mary Slessor and many others did not confine their love to a single household, but God used them to bless the multitudes. They have left the world richer because of their unselfish labors in hospitals, schools, camps, other vocations, and in the home and foreign mission fields.

Christ will not only be your Saviour and friend; but Isaiah 54:5 says, "For thy Maker is thine husband; the Lord of hosts is his name." Every Christian is a part of the bride of Christ. How wonderful to be able to sing,

> **Jesus, Lover of my soul,**
> **Let me to Thy bosom fly.**

I cannot think of finer, greater words than, "Christ died for our sins" (I Cor. 15:3). Though we are sinful, unworthy and unlovely, He loves us with an everlasting love. He says, "I will never leave thee, nor forsake thee," and He is the same yesterday and today and forever.

> **He loves me, He loves me;**
> **Oh, the wonder of such a thought,**
> **That He loves me;**
> **He loves me, He loves me;**
> **I never could love Him the way I ought,**
> **But He loves me.**

Have you given Christ your all? He is anxious to lift every burden, solve every problem, answer every question, and supply your every need. He will give you power to be the spiritual mother of many. His way is the best and only way that counts for time and for eternity. Will you pray this prayer every day? "Lord, help me to know Thy will, to love Thy will, and to do Thy will for my life." Are you willing to yield your all upon His altar and let Him choose everything for you?

I dare not choose my lot;
  I would not if I might.
Choose Thou for me, my God,
  So I shall walk aright.

The kingdom that I seek
  Is Thine; so let the way
That leads to it be Thine,
  Else surely I might stray.

Take Thou my cup, and it
  With joy or sorrow fill;
As best to Thee may seem,
  Choose Thou my good and ill.

Choose Thou for me my friends,
  My sickness and my health;
Choose Thou my cares for me,
  My poverty or wealth.

Not mine—not mine the choice,
  In things both great and small,
Be Thou my Guide, my Strength,
  My Wisdom and my ALL.
           —H. BONAR

CHAPTER III

A GOD-GUIDED LOVE AFFAIR

To marry without divine guidance is a sin and tragedy. If more people prayed earnestly about their love affairs, the divorce mill would not be so busy grinding out broken homes. Be sure that your prayers are unselfish when you present them to God. One girl, the only child in the family, prayed, "Oh, Lord, I am not asking for anything for myself; but please send my mother a son-in-law!" Another girl said, "Lord, I'm willing to marry either John or Jim, just so it's John!"

I prayerfully suggest five "Don'ts" and five "Do's" in connection with marriage.

DON'T MARRY FOR MONEY

You cannot buy happiness with gold and silver. Money cannot buy the things that make life worthwhile. Some of the saddest people in the world are very wealthy. Some of the happiest people on earth are living in poverty. Money can buy a house, but money cannot purchase a home. Money can buy a wife, but money cannot purchase the love of a wife.

Some girls marry for a home, meal ticket and beautiful clothes. It is exceedingly dangerous to get your eyes fixed on the material things of life.

"But they that will be rich fall into temptation and a snare, and into many foolish and hurtful lusts, which drown men in destruction and perdition. For the love of money is the root of all evil: which while some coveteth after, they have erred from the faith, and pierced themselves through with many sorrows."—I Tim. 6:9, 10.

"Love not the world, neither the things that are in the world. If any man love the world, the love of the Father is not in him."—I John 2:15.

"Lay not up for yourselves treasures upon earth, where moth and rust doth corrupt, and where thieves break through and steal: But lay up for yourselves treasures in heaven, where neither moth nor rust doth corrupt, and where thieves do not break through nor steal: For where your treasure is, there will your heart be also."—Matt. 6:19–21.

A lady once told me how she had two suitors: one rich, the other poor. She had to make a choice, and she chose the poor man because she really loved him. Here is her testimony:

"The money was a big temptation because I have always been poor. I have never regretted my choice because God has given us a happy home built on love for Christ and love for each other. He showed me that wealth can never take the place of love. No girl should ever be deceived into marrying a man just because he has money."

DON'T MARRY BECAUSE IT'S POPULAR

It is possible for marriage to become a fad. Don't ever get the idea that your engagement must be announced immediately just because the majority of your friends are getting married. Remember, some people marry because it affords an entry into social circles, and others marry entirely because of physical attraction.

Many girls have fancied they were in love just because they desired above everything else to get married. A young lady was asked, "What do you prefer most in a man: wealth, education or appearance?" She quickly responded, "Appearance; and the quicker he appears, the better!" One girl confessed that she was two-thirds married: "I have my consent and the preacher's," she explained.

A girl said to me after a women's service, "Until I heard that message, I had the idea that every girl was supposed to get married. I have come very near marrying the wrong man. I am determined to break up with him and go back to college and get my degree. Most of my friends are either married or engaged, and I thought that I must do the same thing. From now on I'll let the Lord lead me as He would have me go." She did finish college with high honors and today is happily married and working for her Saviour.

DON'T MARRY AN EXTREMELY JEALOUS MAN

Jealousy has probably broken up more homes than anything else. There must be mutual trust for a home to be harmonious. If your boyfriend won't trust you before you are married, do you think he will trust you afterwards? The wedding ceremony does not eliminate this green-eyed monster called Jealousy. You are headed for plenty of trouble when you marry an extremely jealous man.

Jealousy is "suspicious fear or watchfulness." The Bible gives us a remedy for this fear that constitutes jealousy. "There is no fear in love; but perfect love casteth out fear: because fear hath torment. He that feareth is not made perfect in love" (I John 4:18).

When a couple really loves Christ and each other, they can certainly trust each other. There is a big question about the genuineness of a love that is accompanied by jealousy.

DON'T MARRY A LAZY MAN

A very "unselfish" fellow once boasted that he intended to marry a working girl and give her half of her salary. Some poor unfortunates don't even rate a fifty percent basis. If you marry a lazy stick wearing pants, you may have to work hard to "make the dough" as well as "bake the dough." Instead of supporting one, you will have two on your weary hands. This procedure can be called jumping out of the frying pan into the fire.

There are times when, through choice or of necessity, the wife works outside the home; but it is a sad story when she must do it because of a good-for-nothing, lazy outfit called a husband.

It may seem difficult for every deserving man to get employment under our present economic system, but many men are so lazy they'd rather "pull for the handout" than to work after "punching the clock." If you are even keeping company with a man like this, you had better give him his walking papers at once. No man is worthy of you who will not give his best for your support, protection and happiness.

DON'T MARRY AN UNSAVED MAN

Some foolish girls marry men hoping to reform them. A girl once told me how she planned to reform a fellow after marriage, who drank and had other evil habits. I asked her, "If you had those habits, do you think he would be foolish enough to marry you, hoping to reform you?" "I really hadn't thought about it from that standpoint," she replied.

Do you remember that very important verse in the preceding chapter? "Be ye not unequally yoked together with unbelievers: for what fellowship hath righteousness with unrighteousness? and what communion hath light with darkness?" (II Cor. 6:14).

Instead of the man being reformed by the woman, he oftentimes pulls her down to his standards, and she is soon living in sin with him. If he will not attend church with you regularly before you are married, it is doubtful that he will afterward. And another thing—beware of the fellow who goes to church with you just because you want him to go. The question is: Does he go for your sake or Christ's sake?

Some boys will profess to become a Christian in order to win the hand and heart of a good Christian girl. Be sure he gets converted to Christ and not just to you. You should know that he "possesses salvation" and not just "professes religion" to get into the good graces of you or your family. You cannot afford to make the awful mistake or take the tragic chance of standing at the altar with an unsaved man by your side.

DO MARRY A MAN YOU LOVE

Every girl courts disaster when she becomes

engaged to a man for any reason but true love. Unless the love is genuine and abiding, there will be three rings connected with the wedding instead of two. I refer to the engagement ring, the wedding ring and the "suffe-ring." Don't forget that it takes love mortar to hold a home together.

Fascination or admiration must not be taken or mistaken for true love. It is easy for girls to be swept off their feet by strong, talented or handsome men. Even though a miracle happened, and you should "make a go" of married life, there can be no real joy without real love. This type of husband will probably give a formal and occasional demonstration of affection. He may even kiss his wife when he comes home, but it is merely a habit such as wiping his feet on the door mat. He may seem warmhearted and nice in public, and yet cold-blooded and cruel in the privacy of their house—not home. She is more of a slave than a wife.

When love is pure, it will not be taken for granted after the wedding day; but through cultivation it will grow stronger and lovelier as the years go by. The honeymoon should continue through life. One man remarked, "Well, the 'moon' doesn't always shine, but my `honey' gets sweeter all the time!" If you desire that kind of a lifelong honeymoon, be sure that you're sure that you're *sure* that he loves you, and know that you know that you *know* that you love him!

True love is the uniting of two hearts into one heart by the divine Lover, the Lord Jesus Christ. When this is accomplished, they will be able to march harmoniously down life's pathway. This kind of love takes them "together as one" through sorrow or joy, poverty or wealth, the rough or smooth, sickness or health, and life or death. This kind of love continues throughout the ceaseless ages of eternity.

Do Marry a Considerate Man

A wise man will check up on a woman's cooking and sewing ability before he marries her. In fact, there are many things upon which he had better check. Some men have unfortunately married women who were "quite pretty," but "awfully dumb." One fellow said, "I will" and "I do" in response to the minister's questions relative to a young lady by his side who could not cook. She soon developed into a professional can opener and green salad maker. He got terribly tired of the green stuff and desperately declared, "My dear, who do you think I am—a goose or a cow?

One man came home to find his young wife weeping. "What is the matter?" he asked sympathetically. Between her sobs she replied, "I baked my first cake today, and Fido sneaked in and ate it right off the table." "Don't cry, dear. I'll buy you another little dog!" He figured that the cake had killed Fido!

A girl should also do some checking up on a boy before she becomes his bride. She should know about the consideration shown his mother, sisters and friends. If he is not considerate of others, will he be considerate of his wife? Consideration is like a smile; it costs very little, but it does more good than words can express.

Real consideration helps to eliminate selfishness and thoughtlessness. It plays a great part in the building of a happy home. Your husband should have a constant regard for your well-being, and he should be careful and thoughtful even in little things.

DO MARRY A CONGENIAL MAN

A happily married woman once said, "I not only married a husband, but I married a pal. We really enjoy going to the same places, doing the same things, and conversing on the same subjects. Of course, he has his hobbies, and I have mine; but there is a mutual interest and understanding in them."

There are some exceptions, but in most cases it is better for college girls to marry college boys. Some gain a general education through travel or home study which may be more practical than a degree from some colleges, but the thing to remember is that a couple should not be too unequally yoked even from an intellectual standpoint.

How can a home be really happy unless the husband and wife are congenial? The word *congenial* means "kindred, cognate, pleasant and sympathetic." Without these things you can expect antagonism, disagreements and misunderstanding. I don't know a better place than the home to apply the famous saying, "United we stand; divided we fall!"

DO MARRY A CHRISTIAN MAN

"If I can't marry a man who is a real Christian, I will never be married," said a wise young woman. A Christian girl should never even consider getting serious with a man who is not saved. We read an important question in Amos 3:3: "Can two walk together, except they be agreed?" There may be differences about some things, but there must be perfect agreement concerning Christ and His Word if there is to be peace and harmony in a home.

Be sure that you marry a man who puts Christ first in everything. You cannot trust a man who is not a yielded Christian. It takes Christ to make a man or woman do what they should do, say what they should say, and be what they should be. If you live alone, you must have Christ, or life is not worth living. If you have a companion, both of you must have Christ, or life is incomplete and a miserable failure. If you ever marry, be sure to marry a child of God.

DO MARRY IN GOD'S WILL

You should be sure that you are in the center of God's will before you establish a home. For surrendered Christians I firmly believe the old adage, "Marriages are made in heaven." If it is God's will for you to be married and have a home, He has a partner for you somewhere. Be patient; live each moment as He would have you live; and in His own good time, He will see to it that your partner, of His choosing, will cross your path. Things will be made clear as you trust Him and "follow step by step."

I have known several girls to break their engagements after being converted or making a complete surrender to Christ. Some have never married, and others married at a later date to a man of God's choice. One girl said to me, "I realize that I should not marry that man, but can I afford to send the ring back and break the engagement?" I replied, "It is a choice between breaking the engagement now or having your heart and home broken later on. God give you grace to make the right decision." The ring was returned the following day with the message: "After much prayer, I know that God is not in our plans. From henceforth and forever—it is all off!"

The Bible plainly teaches that the Holy Spirit is the Guide for yielded Christians. If you are unsaved or even defeated in your Christian life, you cannot expect this divine guidance. He wants to guide every detail of our lives.

"Howbeit when he, the Spirit of truth, is come, he will guide you into all truth; for he shall not speak of himself; but whatsoever he shall hear, that shall he speak: and he will show you things to come."—John 16:13.

"So they, being sent forth by the Holy Ghost, departed unto Seleucia; and from thence they sailed to Cyprus."—Acts 13:4.

"Now when they had gone throughout Phrygia and the region of Galatia, and were forbidden of the Holy Ghost to preach the word in Asia, After they were come to Mysia, they assayed to go into Bithynia: but the Spirit suffered them not."—Acts 16:6, 7.

"But the Comforter, which is the Holy Ghost, whom the Father will send in my name, he shall teach you all things, and bring all things to your remembrance, whatsoever I have said unto you."—John 14:26.

"Trust in the Lord with all thine heart; and lean not unto thine own understanding. In all thy ways acknowledge him, and he shall direct thy paths."—Prov. 3:5, 6.

"If any of you lack wisdom, let him ask of God, that

giveth to all men liberally, and upbraideth not; and it shall be given him."—Jas. 1:5.

"Delight thyself also in the Lord; and he shall give thee the desires of thine heart. Commit thy way unto the Lord; trust also in him; and he shall bring it to pass...The steps of a good man are ordered by the Lord: and he delighteth in his way."—Ps. 37:4, 5, 23.

HE KEEPS THE KEY

Is there some problem in your life to solve,
  Some passage seeming full of mystery?
God knows, who brings the hidden things to light;
  He keeps the key.

Is there some door closed by the Father's hand
  Which widely opened you had hoped to see;
Trust God and wait—for when He shuts the door,
  He keeps the key.

Is there some earnest prayer unanswered yet,
  Or answered NOT as you had hoped 'twould be?
God will make clear His purpose by-and-by;
  He keeps the key.

Unfailing comfort, sweet and blessed rest,
  To know of EVERY door He keeps the key;
That He at last, when just He sees 'tis best,
  Will give it thee.

Chapter IV

HOME

What Makes It and What Breaks It

The word "HOME" always stirs our memories. For those who had a happy Christian home, the word is exceedingly precious. Home was the first institution established by the hand of God. It came before the church, school, government or anything else. God places a great premium on the home, and we need to remember that society cannot rise higher than the home. In fact, the home is the very foundation of civilization.

This chapter is written for men and women, boys and girls. I trust that you will encourage every member of your family to read it carefully and prayerfully.

What Makes a Home

There are many things that help to make a home, but I can only mention five in this short chapter.

True Love

If we love Christ with all our heart, we will have a

tender love for every member of our family. Christ should be the very center of our home. He should be the hub of the wheel of our home, and every spoke must head up in Him if there is to be success and harmony.

Love for Christ and for each other seems to make the hard places softer, the rough places smoother, the problems less difficult, the questions easier, and the burdens lighter. A little girl almost staggered under the weight of a fat baby. Someone said, "Isn't that baby too heavy for you?" She quickly replied, "Oh no, he's not too heavy. You see, he's my brother." Love makes the difference, doesn't it? Love mortar is the best kind to hold a home together.

THE STICK-TOGETHER FAMILIES

The stick-together families are happier by far
Than the brothers and sisters who take separate highways are.
The gladdest people living are the wholesome folks who make
A circle at the fireside that no power but death can break.
And the finest of conventions ever held beneath the sun
Are the little family gatherings when the busy day is done.
There are rich folk, there are poor folk, who imagine they
          are wise,
And they're very quick to shatter all the little family ties.
Each goes searching after pleasure in his own selected way;
Each with strangers likes to wander, and with strangers
          likes to play.
But it's bitterness they harvest, and it's empty joy they find;
For the children that are wisest are the stick-together kind.
There are some who seem to fancy that for gladness they
          must roam;
That for smiles that are the brightest, they must wander far
          from home;
That the strange friend is the true friend, and they travel
          far astray,

And they waste their lives in striving for a joy that's far away.
But the gladdest sort of people, when the busy day is done,
Are the brothers and sisters who together share their fun.
It's the stick-together family that wins the joys of earth,
That hears the sweetest music and that finds the finest mirth.
It's the old home roof that shelters all the charm that life
    can give;
There you find the gladdest playground; there, the happiest
    spot to live.
And O weary, wandering brother, if contentment you
    would win,
Come you back unto the fireside and be comrade with
    your kin.

—EDGAR A. GUEST
(From Just Folks. Copyrighted by The Reilly
& Lee Co., Chicago. Used by permission.)

FAMILY ALTAR

A young married woman once said to me, "My husband and I started a family altar the first night after we were married. Reading the Bible and praying together has been such a blessing to us. We would not cease having our altar for anything in the world."

Many people have told me similar stories. My wife and I can add our testimony to the blessings received at the family altar. We started ours the night we were married. Now, usually after the evening meal, we retire to the living room and read two verses each until we finish a chapter in the Bible, and then kneel for prayer. We all pray each time. In this way we are drawn closer to each other and to the Lord. We also have private devotions in the morning.

Why don't you parents establish, or reestablish, an altar in your home? You cheat yourselves and your children out of a great blessing if you neglect this valuable institution. I have known young people and children to desire a family altar so much that their parents established one because of their persistence. Do you have the altar in your home?

IF EVERY HOME WERE AN ALTAR

If every home were an altar
  Where the holiest vows were paid
And life's best gifts in sacrament
  Of purest love were laid;

If every home were an altar
  Where harsh and angry thought
Were cast aside for kindly one
  And true forgiveness sought;

If every home were an altar
  Where hearts weighed down with care
Could find sustaining strength and grace
  In sweet uplift and prayer;

Then solved would be earth's problems,
  Banished sin's curse and blight,
For God's own love would radiate
  From every altar light.

CONSISTENT CHRISTIAN LIVING

This includes unselfishness, consideration, forgiveness, patience, and many other things. Inconsistency is one of the worst sins in the catalog. Do the members of your family have confidence in your Christianity and respect for your testimony? Can they see Christ in your every word and deed? They may not read the Bible, but they read your life every day. Are you demonstrating that Christ saves, keeps and satisfies?

"Let your light so shine before men, that they may see your good works, and glorify your Father which is in heaven."— Matt. 5:16.

TACTFUL AUTHORITY

Many parents are not tactful in their discipline. They do not seem to realize the possibility of being firm and kind at the same time. You may get suggestions from books of psychology, but God alone can give you the necessary wisdom in rearing your children.

There were two things in our home that I will never forget: the Bible that my father used at night, and the razor strop which he used—well, quite frequently. As a boy I thought my father was terribly unkind to the peach trees that grew in our back yard. He would snatch off the larger sprouts and damage was not only done to the trees, but in other quarters as well.

The older I get, the more I appreciate that "razor-strop soup" and that "peach sprout tonic." I am indeed grateful that my father could say an emphatic "No!" His example and good advice did more for me than words can express.

"And ye fathers, provoke not your children to wrath: but bring them up in the nurture and admonition of the Lord."—Eph. 6:4.

LOVING OBEDIENCE

The best place to learn to obey is at home. It will come natural for us to obey the rules at school and the laws of the land if we learn obedience at home. Young man, young lady, there will come a time in your life when you will deeply regret every disobedient act, every unkind word, every bit of trouble, and every anxious moment you caused your parents.

"Children, obey your parents in the Lord: for this is right. Honour thy father and mother; which is the first commandment with promise; That it may be well with thee, and thou mayest live long on the earth."—Eph. 6:1–3.

The secret is found in obeying and loving Christ. It may be that your parents and friends have prayed earnestly for you, and you are still unsaved. If you have not been genuinely converted, I beg you to accept the Lord Jesus Christ as your personal Saviour this very day. This decision is too important to postpone.

"But as many as received him, to them gave he power to become the sons of God, even to them that believe on his name."—John 1:12.

"He that hath the Son hath life; and he that hath not the Son of God hath not life."—I John 5:12.

WHAT BREAKS A HOME?

We all know that one little word spelled with three little letters is the cause of all the broken homes, blighted hopes, wrecked ambitions, and all the other trouble in the world. That word is *sin*.

The following verses give some valuable information about marriage and the home:

"The Pharisees also came unto him, tempting him, and saying unto him, Is it lawful for a man to put away his wife for every cause? And he answered and said unto them, Have ye not read, that he which made them at the beginning made them male and female, And said, For this cause

shall a man leave father and mother, and shall cleave to his wife: and they twain shall be one flesh? Wherefore they are no more twain, but one flesh. What therefore God hath joined together, let not man put asunder. They say unto him, Why did Moses then command to give a writing of divorcement, and to put her away? He saith unto them, Moses because of the hardness of your hearts suffered you to put away your wives: but from the beginning it was not so. And I say unto you, Whosoever shall put away his wife, except it be for fornication, and shall marry another, com-mitteth adultery: and whoso marrieth her which is put away doth commit adultery."—Matt. 19:3–9.

"Wives, submit yourselves unto your own husbands, as unto the Lord. For the husband is the head of the wife, even as Christ is the head of the church: and he is the saviour of the body. Therefore as the church is subject unto Christ, so let the wives be to their own husbands in every thing. Husbands, love your wives, even as Christ also loved the church, and gave himself for it."—Eph. 5:22–25.

"For this cause shall a man leave his father and mother, and shall be joined unto his wife, and they two shall be one flesh. This is a great mystery: but I speak concerning Christ and the church. Nevertheless let every one of you in partic-ular so love his wife even as himself; and the wife see that she reverence her husband."—Eph. 5:31–33.

It is a sad fact that so many marriages are broken by divorces. Someone asked a movie actress, "Are you married?" She smilingly replied, "Yes, occasionally." A divorce is a sad and dangerous thing every way you figure it.

I will discuss briefly five of the many things used by

the Devil to break homes and hearts.

SELFISHNESS

It is easy for selfish people to become stubborn, and what a combination! There is plenty of giving and taking, and sometimes it seems that the "for worse" exceeds the "for better." Too many folks want to have their own way whether it be right or wrong.

Some couples would like to have their home blessed with children, but sometimes this is denied. Others selfishly refuse to accept the responsibility of a family, when one or more children might do more to weld the home together and bring real joy than anything else.

If people are unselfish, yielded Christians, the Holy Spirit will enable them to solve aright every problem of their home. Only selfish people prevent the Lord Jesus Christ from being

> **The Heart of the house,**
> **The unseen Guest at every meal,**
> **And the silent Listener to every conversation.**

INTEMPERANCE

This word, according to Mr. Webster, means "want of moderation or self-restraint; excess, especially in the use of alcoholic liquors."

Good habits and bad habits are easily formed, but bad ones are especially hard to break. There are some habits which would not necessarily break a home, but should be left off if they are expensive, injurious to health, or a bad influence upon our family or others.

We should not be intemperate in our eating. I once heard of a man who was told by his doctor to quit eating so many sweets. He was especially warned about pies, just the thing he loved better than anything else. As many others, he would not watch his diet; and after digging his grave with his teeth, this inscription was written on his tomb:

> **He couldn't say no to whipped cream pie,**
> **And for that reason here he doth lie.**

The use of tobacco is one of the most expensive and pointless habits of all. Why will folks throw away money for something that injures their health? If for no other reason, economy and health should prevent any person from using tobacco in any form. When older people use it, they certainly are not setting a good example for children and young people.

> **Tobacco is a filthy weed.**
> **It was the Devil who sowed the seed.**
> **It picks your pockets, spoils your clothes,**
> **And makes a chimney out of your nose.**

It is not my purpose to enumerate the habits of which people are guilty, but I must say something about strong drink. There are some things that we can afford to partake of in a temperate way, but other things should never be touched at all. Everyone should know that alcohol comes in this latter class. War has killed millions, but whiskey has killed tens of millions and broken many, many homes.

Selfish folks argue that they must have it for medical purposes, and they stubbornly excuse their "Christmas toddy" and "the social drink." People get sick very quickly and quite frequently when the "peppy tonic" is waiting close by. Some say, "Oh, I can take it or leave it!" They usually take it too, and seldom ever leave it.

We read in Proverbs 20:1:

"Wine is a mocker, strong drink is raging; and whosoever is deceived thereby is not wise."

We need a heart purpose as Daniel had.

"But Daniel purposed in his heart that he would not defile himself with the portion of the king's meat, nor with the wine which he drank."—Dan. 1:8.

If you have never started these bad habits, don't ever start! If you are in the grip of any of them, remember, there is liberty in the Lord Jesus Christ.

"If the Son therefore shall make you free, ye shall be free indeed."—John 8:36.

"Therefore if any man be in Christ, he is a new creature: old things are passed away; behold, all things are become new."—II Cor. 5:17.

DISLOYALTY

It is worse than a crime for people to break the sacred vows of marriage. Your vows were made not only in the presence of witnesses, but also in the presence of Almighty God. It is better never to make a promise than to make one and break it. We would have sympathy but not respect for any man or woman who breaks his solemn oath, and I wonder if they can have any self-respect.

A man in a northern city came to my hotel room and requested prayer. Here is his story: "I met a girl at church. She sang in the choir. After some months of courtship, we were married. I almost worshiped that girl and lived true to her every minute. She left me recently and went away with another man. I didn't dream that there was anything wrong until the tragedy had happened."

I once visited a very humble home with a Christian woman who took some food to some hungry children. One little fellow about six was ill. His sister, not more than ten, was acting as mother and nursemaid. A child of three years played on the floor. The father was working; and the mother had gotten in trouble with another married man, and both had left the country. Two homes were broken, and several hearts were crushed. Just another sad picture painted by the slimy brush of disloyalty.

In a southern city a grief-stricken mother said to me: "Please pray for my husband. I know that he is not true to me, and our home is on the very verge of being broken. I never nag and would never think of being disloyal in any way. How I wish that he would be converted and live right for the sake of the children and the family name."

MISUNDERSTANDING

If the machinery of the home runs smoothly, the oil of sympathetic understanding must be applied constantly. This oil will take you speedily over the ups and downs along the path of life.

Hearts are very easily broken because they are very tender. It is hard to mend one when it is broken.

Neither husband nor wife should be too selfish and

proud to say, "Please forgive me; I am sorry." Some folks should think, not twice, but many times before they speak. A couple should try to understand each other's background, temperament, and problems. She should be willing to help him with his letters, and he should be only too glad to don an apron and assist in doing the dishes. Marriage that is not built on a oneness or together-proposition is certain to go on the rocks.

They were so truly one
That no one knew which ruled and which obeyed.
He ruled because she would obey,
And she, by loving, ruled the most.

A friend of mine in England tells the story of a couple who had quarreled, and they slowly walked down the road several feet apart. "What words is that bird in the tree singing?" asked the man. "I can't imagine," responded his wife. "It is singing, 'I love you, I love you, I love you.'" Both were quiet a few steps, and she said, "There is another bird. Can you guess what it is singing?"

"I don't know," he replied. "It is singing, 'Show it, show it, show it'!" He did show it; and instead of living "scrappily," they lived "happily ever after."

JEALOUSY

The poets call jealousy "a green-eyed monster." It is worse than that; jealousy crushes confidence and trust under its wicked heel. It works overtime in breaking homes and hearts. Jealousy destroys affections; undermines harmony; breaks the closest bonds; and in the words of an old saying, "is as cruel as the grave."

There is only one cure for jealousy, that is, both

hearts loving Christ supremely and trusting each other completely. If both parties are genuinely converted and live a yielded Christian life, there will be no room for jealousy in their hearts. If you keep Christ the head of your life and home, the Devil will never be able to break it up.

A HOUSE OR HOME?

It takes more than a house to make a home. You can live in a palace and have only a house. You can live in a rented flat, humble cottage or small cabin and have a real home. It is easy to transform a home into a mere boarding house, just a place to eat and sleep. Do you live in a house or a home?

A Christian home is the nearest thing on earth to Heaven. It has been called an annex to the Glory Land. You parents have a right, by faith, to claim every member of your family for Christ and heaven. "Believe on the Lord Jesus Christ, and thou shalt be saved, and thy house" (Acts 16:31). Parents should go in for household salvation.

If a wife will live consistently, she can win her husband and children to Christ. It may take time, but do not get discouraged. Many consecrated men have won their wives to the Saviour. Parents can have the assurance that the family circle will be unbroken in the sky. Do not stop praying and working until every child is in the fold.

After the funeral of an elderly woman who had been left a widow early in life, a neighbor asked the eldest of six sons, "How did she do it?" He took her to his mother's room and pointed to an old chair and rug. Two dents could be seen in the rug where the mother had knelt to pray each day for many years. "Prayer is the secret," he said. "It is the thing that brought us through every hard place. We boys were wayward at times, but she never stopped praying. Through her earnest prayers and godly influence, she won all of us boys to her Saviour."

Do you live a life of prayer? Do you have in your home that priceless institution called the family altar? Can the other members of your family and the neighbors see Christ in your daily walk? Won't you say with the prophet, "As for me and my house, we will serve the Lord"? (Josh. 24:15).

Chapter V

THE RESPONSIBILITY OF MOTHERHOOD

UPON YOU MOTHERS rests the greatest responsibility in the world. Your job is that of molding lives and shaping character. There is dignity, honor, privilege and responsibility in your position as a mother. God expects you to raise your children for Him. How any mother can live in sin and not be a Christian is more than I can understand.

Once during a conversation, a woman asked, "How soon should a young mother start praying for her child?" An old family physician happened to be in the group, and he replied, "Twenty years before it is born." The young mother's prayer in the poem by Fay Inchfawn is very touching.

MOTHER, I'M COMING
I heard you, Sweet! And I'll prepare,
So lovingly, your dainty wear.
Oh, I will dream and scheme each day;
And planning, put the pence away.

Then too not only will I make
Soft woolly comforts for your sake;
But I will fashion, if I can,
Fine raiment for your inner man.
I will not think on evil things
Lest I should clip my darling's wings.
I'll set my heart to understand
The great Salvation God has planned.
Yes, every atom of my being;
All feeling, tasting, hearing, seeing;
He shall refine and garnish too.
I'll be God's woman through and through.
Lord, take me; and if this may be,
Possess my little child through me!

I heard the story once about a mother who went to a circus, and while standing by a bear pit feeding the bears, her little baby wiggled out of her arms and fell into the midst of the hungry bears. The baby's body was quickly torn to shreds. The child was lost because she neglected her responsibility and was careless in holding her child. If you mothers are not careful, your boys and girls will fall into the pit of sin, and their immortal souls will be lost. My earnest prayer is that every mother who reads this message will realize fully her great responsibility.

My mother died when I was ten years old. However, before she died, she taught me to say my little prayers, and she told me of Jesus and His love. I am sure that her earnest prayers led to my conversion when I was sixteen and to my surrender to preach the Gospel two years later. Oh, memories of mother—sweet music of the past!

Among the treasured pictures
  That I've hung on memory's wall,
There's one that's clearer than the rest
  And sweeter far than all:
'Tis a picture of my mother
  When I, a little chap,
Was folded in her loving arms,
  To slumber on her lap.
I felt her hands caress my head;
  I heard her softly say,
"Dear Jesus, take this little life
  And use it every day."

There must have been a mighty weight
  Behind that simple prayer,
For through the seasons, year on year,
  The picture lingers there.
And whether I'm on hill or plain
  Or on the deep blue sea,
The memory of that sacred scene
  Forever comforts me:
Among the treasured pictures
  That I've hung on memory's wall,
My mother's supplication
  Is the sweetest one of all.

Someone has said that God couldn't be everywhere at the same time so He has given us mothers. Of course, we know that God is everywhere; He is omnipresent; but that is a beautiful tribute to motherhood.

Two people very dear to Jesus were standing at the foot of the cross: Mary, His mother; and John, the beloved disciple. In that great and awful hour Jesus was not unmindful of His mother. He committed her to the care of John. In the hour of His greatest conflict He thought of His mother's service and love and made provision for her necessities. If we will follow the example of Jesus, we will never forget mother.

It is impossible to find fitting words to describe a good mother.

> If I could write with diamond pen,
>   Use ink of flowing gold,
> The love I have for my mother dear,
>   Could then not half be told.
>
> Her sympathy has been my stay;
>   Her love, my guiding light;
> Her gentle hand hath soothed my ills;
>   She's ever guided right.
>
> A precious friend has mother been,
>   Stood by me all the way,
> No sacrifice has been too great,
>   Such love one can't repay.
>
> So wonderful has Mother been,
>   So gentle, kind and good,
> That I have learned to reverence
>   That sweet word *motherhood.*

The word *mother* is one of the most beautiful words in our language. It is one of the first words that we learn to say. There is power in this dear word. I once read the story of a burglar who returned a stolen watch to the owner because he could not stand to see on the back of the watch the words, "To Son, from Mother, on his birthday."

> No painter's brush or poet's pen,
> In justice to her fame,
> Has ever reached half high enough
> To write my mother's name.

Make ink of tears and golden gems
And sunbeams mixed together;
With holy hand and golden pen,
Go write the name of Mother.

In every humble tenant house,
In every cottage home,
In marble courts and gilded halls
And on every palace dome,

On mountains high, in valleys low,
In every land and clime,
On every throbbing human heart,
That blessed name enshrine.

Take childhood's light and manhood's age,
Celestial canvas given,
In beauty trace her name and face,
And go hang it up in Heaven.

Thrice upward to the heavenly Home,
And midst music soft and sweet,
Thank Jesus for your Mother's name,
And write it at His feet.

Thank God for what consecrated, praying, Christian mothers have meant to the world. The most influential person on earth is a mother. After a young man accepted Christ and joined the church, his pastor asked him what part of his message made him want to live a Christian life. The young man answered, "Nothing that you said, but the way my mother lived in our home." It was not preaching but practicing that won him.

There was once a young man in a penitentiary who refused to take his mother's picture when it was offered him. He replied, "I don't want her picture. I am in this place today because of her influence. She taught me to play cards in our home, and I became a gambler and committed the crime that put me here for life."

Susanna Wesley was the mother of nineteen children. "I raised my children to be Christians by getting hold of their hearts when they were young and never losing my grip," said Mrs. Wesley.

The following statement was made by John Randolph in the House of Representatives: "Today I would be an infidel if it had not been for my godly mother." No truer statement was ever uttered than the statement, "The hand that rocks the cradle is the hand that rules the world."

A mother in west Florida told me the story of how she went into her garden to work one day, and when she looked around, she saw her little girl taking long steps. She said, "Nell, what are you doing?" The little girl replied, "I am stepping in your tracks, Mother. I know if I step in your tracks, I won't get thorns in my feet." This mother said that she prayed right there that God would help her to be a true Christian so her boys and girls could follow her to Heaven.

A dying boy said to his mother, "I am going home now to see Jesus, Mother, and I am going to tell Jesus that you told me how to live for Him." Mothers, are you living a true, consistent, Christian life every day? Are you pointing your children to Heaven?

THE BRAVERY OF MOTHER

A good mother is the bravest person on earth. She forgets her own welfare when her children are in danger. She will sacrifice her very life if need be for her children. It takes bravery to fight the battles of life that a mother fights.

> The bravest battle that was ever fought,
>   Shall I tell you where and when?
> On the maps of the world you'll find it not—
>   'Twas fought by the mothers of men.
>
> Nay, not with cannon or battle shot,
>   With sword or noble pen;
> Nay, not with eloquent word or thought,
>   From the mouths of wonderful men;
>
> But deep in the walled-up woman's heart
>   Of women who would not yield,
> But bravely, silently bore their part—
>   Lo, there is the battlefield.
>
> No marshaling troops, no patriotic song,
>   No banner to gleam and wave;
> But oh, those battles, they last so long,
>   From babyhood to the grave.

THE MUSIC OF MOTHER

The best music in the world is the music that a Christian mother makes as she sings from her heart of love the old hymns. Here is the song that my mother loved to sing:

> 'Tis so sweet to trust in Jesus,
>   Just to take Him at His Word;
> Just to rest upon His promise;
>   Just to know, "Thus saith the Lord."
>
> I'm so glad I learned to trust Thee,
>   Precious Jesus, Saviour, Friend;
> And I know that Thou art with me,
>   Wilt be with me to the end.

In a northern city there were three gamblers who had spent most of the night in sin, when suddenly their conversation turned toward religion. "No one has true religion," said one of the men. "You're right," said another. The other man looked over the card table and said, "Fellows, don't say that; I know we don't have any religion, but some folks have." "Who is it?" asked the other gamblers. He replied, "My wife has genuine religion; and if you don't believe it, follow me, and I'll prove it to you."

He led the way to a humble house on a back street. When he knocked at the door, a sad but sweet-faced woman opened it. It was his wife. With rough language he commanded her to cook them something to eat at that late hour. The men renewed their game of cards as she prepared supper for them. After a few minutes they heard music from the kitchen. She was singing the words of an old hymn:

> **Must Jesus bear the cross alone,**
> **And all the world go free?**
> **No, there's a cross for everyone,**
> **And there's a cross for me.**

One of the gamblers dropped his cards on the table; but before he had time to speak, another verse came floating out:

> **The consecrated cross I'll bear,**
> **Till death shall set me free,**
> **And then go Home my crown to wear,**
> **For there's a crown for me.**

The man who dropped his cards fell on his knees saying, "If that woman has something in her heart that can make her sing like that under these circumstances, she has in her heart what I want in mine."

The other men were under conviction too; so they called this singing mother into the room to pray for them, and they were all converted that night.

THE KISS OF MOTHER

There is courage, hope, ambition and inspiration in the kiss of a Christian mother. Benjamin West became a painter because of the encouraging kiss of his mother. Many boys and girls have accomplished great things for God and humanity because mother kissed them as children and said, "I believe in you, and I know you can do it."

Years ago in an eastern city, according to the testimony of a physician, a little boy's life was saved because his mother, who had been separated from him a long time, kissed him. He started to recover immediately after his mother planted a loving kiss upon his fevered brow.

THE PRAYERS OF MOTHER

Every one hundred percent Christian home has a family altar. At a convenient time each day, the entire family should read the Bible and pray together. My wife and I make it a point to have our devotions in the early morning. The family altar will draw the family closer together and will help to draw each member of the family closer to Christ. Many children are led to Christ around the family altar.

I thank God that my parents had a family altar in our humble home in south Alabama. I learned to love the blessed Bible by hearing my father read it around the fireside at night. We children were taught to pray by our mother when we were very young.

"Now I lay me down to sleep;
I pray the Lord my soul to keep"
Was my childhood's early prayer,
Taught by my mother's love and care.

Many years since then have fled;
Mother slumbers with the dead.
Yet methinks I see her now,
With lovelit eye and holy brow,

As, kneeling by her side to pray,
She gently taught me how to say,
"Now I lay me down to sleep,
I pray the Lord my soul to keep"!

I have met the Lord at the throne of grace in many lands. I have prayed while at work and at play. I have talked to my Father in wagons, bullock carts, buses, automobiles, trains, ships and airplanes; but I agree with the poet when he said that the best place in the world to pray is at mother's knee.

I have worshiped in churches and chapels.
  I have prayed in the busy street.
I have sought my God and have found Him
  Where the waves of the ocean beat.
I have knelt in the silent forest
  In the shade of some ancient tree,
But the dearest of all my altars
  Was raised at my mother's knee.

I have listened to God in His temple.
  I have caught His voice in the crowd.
I have heard Him speak when the breakers
  Were booming long and loud.
Where the winds play soft in the treetops,
  My Father has talked to me;
But I never have heard Him clearer
  Than I did at my mother's knee.

God make me the man of her vision
  And purge me of selfishness!
God keep me true to her standards
  And help me to live to bless!
God hallow the holy impress
  Of the days that used to be,
And keep me a pilgrim forever
  To the shrine at my mother's knee.

THE LOVE OF MOTHER

There is no earthly love like the comforting love of mother. I once heard the story of an angel who left Heaven and came to earth in search of the three most beautiful things that could be found. The angel started back to Heaven with a beautiful flower, the smile of a little girl and a mother's love. The flower and smile soon faded and had to be cast aside. The angel swept through the pearly gates of Heaven, shouting that the mother's love was the only thing found on earth that would retain its beauty from earth to Heaven.

O mother, sweet mother,
There cannot be another
Whose love is as true
And as constant as thine.

In pleasure or trouble
Your love seems to double.
God bless you, dear mother,
Sweet mother of mine.

Your love 'tis a mother's
And is different from others;
It seems like a love
That is truly divine.

Your hugs and caressing
Bring down divine blessing.
God bless you, dear mother,
Sweet mother of mine.

THE LOVE OF CHRIST

I thank God for the power, influence and beauty of a Christian mother's love. Jesus only has a love greater than mother's love. Christ died for us; and if we will trust Him, some sweet day by and by, He will take us Home to Glory where we can live with our Christian relatives and friends throughout eternity.

Are you saved? Do you have the assurance that you have been born again?

"Except a man be born again, he cannot see the kingdom of God."—John 3:3.

"Except ye repent, ye shall all likewise perish."—Luke 13:3.

"For the wages of sin is death; but the gift of God is eternal life through Jesus Christ our Lord."—Rom. 6:23.

"Believe on the Lord Jesus Christ, and thou shalt be saved."—Acts 16:31.

"But as many as received him, to them gave he power to become the sons of God, even to them that believe on his name."—John 1:12.

"If thou shalt confess with thy mouth the Lord Jesus, and shalt believe in thine heart that God hath raised him from the dead, thou shalt be saved. For with the heart man believeth unto righteousness; and with the mouth confession is made unto salvation."—Rom. 10:9, 10.

If you have never been saved, will you immediately make the following decision?

> Being convinced that I am lost and believing that Jesus Christ died on the cross to save me from sin, I now accept Him as my personal Saviour; and with His help I intend to live the Christian life and confess Him before others.

If you have been converted, but realize that you have grown cold and indifferent, or have not made a complete surrender to Christ, will you make this decision?

> I now yield my all to Jesus Christ, and with His help I intend to live a consistent, consecrated, Christian life.

Some time ago I stood by my mother's grave in south Alabama. As the evening shadows were falling, I fell on my knees and whispered this prayer to Jesus:

> **Tell mother I'll be there**
> **In answer to her prayer;**
> **This message, blessed Saviour, to her bear!**
> **Tell mother I'll be there,**
> **Heaven's joys with her to share.**
> **Yes, tell my darling mother,**
> **I'll be there.**

CHAPTER VI

GOD'S IDEAL WOMAN

The dictionary defines the word *ideal* as "conforming to a standard of perfection; existing in imagination only."

It is humanly impossible to live a perfect life; but with God's help and power, you can meet His high standards.

Many books have been written about physical charm, poise and beauty, but I am writing now about the beauty of character. In the thirty-first chapter of Proverbs, we find a perfect example of beautiful, noble womanhood.

I like to think of her as God's crown of creation, possessing twelve beautiful jewels. We notice that she is virtuous, trustworthy, energetic, physically fit, economical, unselfish, prepared, honorable, prudent, lovable, God-fearing and rewarded. Let us briefly examine each of them.

VIRTUOUS

"Who can find a virtuous woman? for her price is far above rubies."—Vs. 10.

I cannot think of anything more valuable than virtue. Someone has said that it would be better to die a million deaths than to live in sin. People exist as sinners, but as Christians they really live. Purity has power and demands respect.

Many girls yield to temptations, let down the bars, and sacrifice upon the altar of lust their priceless virtue. It is a sad picture that fails to see the roses of purity blooming in the cheeks of girls. Sinful lusts soon cut lines of dissipation in their faces.

Christ will give power to walk the only path that counts—the path of purity. To live a pure, Christian life should be the ambition of everyone. "Blessed are the pure in heart: for they shall see God" (Matt. 5:8).

TRUSTWORTHY

"The heart of her husband doth safely trust in her, so that he shall have no need of spoil. She will do him good and not evil all the days of her life."—Prov. 31:11, 12.

What a compliment to say that she is "true blue"! Any man could trust a woman like this. He knows she would never let him down and that she would rather die than betray his trust. She knows how to keep secrets, but no secrets are kept from each other because they are one in everything.

She is understanding, encouraging, sympathetic and tactful. She is not moody, but has a stability that is a constant brace and inspiration to her husband. When temptation comes, she is there to help him be victorious.

Dependability is a lost art with many people. Our motto, *"True to Christ,"* is all-inclusive. When we are loyal to Christ, no one else will suffer for lack of fidelity. "Be thou faithful unto death, and I will give thee a crown of life" (Rev. 2:10).

ENERGETIC

"She seeketh wool, and flax, and worketh willingly with her hands. She is like the merchants' ships; she bringeth her food from afar. She riseth also while it is yet night, and giveth meat to her household, and a portion to her maidens.She considereth a field, and buyeth it: with the fruit of her hands she planteth a vineyard....She layeth her hands to the spindle, and her hands hold the distaff....She maketh fine linen, and selleth it; and delivereth girdles unto the merchant....She looketh well to the ways of her household, and eateth not the bread of idleness."—Prov. 31:13–16, 19, 24, 27.

She is a worker—not a shirker! She is never lazy. Her heart, head, hands, feet—in fact, her entire being—is dedicated to the welfare of her household.

Her Christianity is practical and is expressed in sacrificial service. You will never find her wasting her time at a bridge club because she always has worthwhile things to do. She enjoys her work and, in spite of seeming monotony, performs it with a cheery smile.

"Slothfulness casteth into a deep sleep; and an idle soul shall suffer hunger."—Prov. 19:15.

PHYSICALLY FIT

"She girdeth her loins with strength, and strengtheneth her arms."—Prov. 31:17.

She realizes she must be healthy in order to perform her strenuous duties efficiently. She watches her diet because she knows the truth of the old adage, "Many people dig their graves with their teeth."

In the midst of her tasks she does not forget the importance of taking time out for recreation. A long hike, a fishing trip or some games in the open air with the children has an invigorating effect on her weary body, and not only adds years to her life, but also cuts down on the doctor bill.

God's ideal woman is free from all habits that would injure her physically, mentally or spiritually. She realizes that her body is the temple of the Holy Spirit, and she does her best to make it a fit dwelling place for Him.

"What? know ye not that your body is the temple of the Holy Ghost which is in you, which ye have of God, and ye are not your own? For ye are bought with a price: therefore glorify God in your body, and in your spirit, which are God's."—I Cor. 6:19, 20.

ECONOMICAL

"She perceiveth that her merchandise is good: her candle goeth not out by night."—Prov. 31:18.

She runs her business on a balanced budget, an accomplishment which is reached by very few governments. She gets good things, in fact the best, but she knows the value of money and how to spend it. She would rather do without some things than to burden the family with difficult installments and staggering debts.

You would almost think that this woman was a magician because she has learned to make old things look new again. You would also be surprised to know that a lovely meal had been prepared from left-overs.

The word *waste* is not in her vocabulary.

"A penny saved is a penny earned," said Benjamin Franklin, and this statement is a thrifty reality in the home of God's ideal woman.

UNSELFISH

"She stretcheth out her hand to the poor; yea, she reacheth forth her hands to the needy."—Prov. 31:20.

Can you blame the neighbors for loving her? The aged, sick and shut-ins find in her their best friend. She is never too busy with her own affairs to rush to the assistance of others. She seems to know when someone is in need and either takes or sends the necessities. Her words bring comfort, hope and cheer to many people along life's way.

"And whosoever will be chief among you, let him be your servant."—Matt. 20:27.

"God loveth a cheerful giver."—II Cor. 9:7.

Her philosophy is expressed in this poem:

Lord, help me live from day to day
In such a self-forgetful way,
That even when I kneel to pray,
My prayers will be for others.

Help me in all the work I do
To ever be sincere and true,
And know that all I do for You
Must needs be done for others.

Let self be crucified and slain
And buried deep, and all in vain
May efforts be to rise again,
Unless to live for others.

And when my work on earth is done
And my new work in Heaven's begun,
May I forget the crown I've won,
While thinking still of others.

Others, Lord, yes, others:
Let this my motto be.
Help me to live for others,
That I may live like Thee.

PREPARED

"She is not afraid of the snow for her household; for all her household are clothed with scarlet. She maketh herself coverings of tapestry; her clothing is silk and purple."—Prov. 31:21, 22.

She knows that the winds of winter will blow and that the earth will be covered with a blanket of snow, but she and her family are ready for it. Let us peep into her pantry and see the delicious fruits and vegetables canned and stored away. Her foresight protects her when the rainy days come.

She is prepared for life and for death because she knows the Saviour. People with true wisdom always make proper preparation for the inevitable. We should all adopt the Scouts' motto, "Be prepared!"

"Prepare to meet thy God."—Amos 4:12.

HONORABLE

"Strength and honour are her clothing."—Prov. 31:25.

The style for this outfit was designed, not in Paris or Hollywood, but in Heaven. The poor can enjoy garments made of these eternal fabrics, strength and honor, just the same as the rich.

God's ideal woman keeps her clothing spotless. Strength and honor can be soiled and spoiled very quickly by Satan. She abstains from the very appearance of evil. She can blush, and she knows what it means for a woman to be modest.

She has divine strength and can stand alone if necessary. She has strong convictions about right and wrong. She does not follow the crowd or do things just because it happens to be customary. She knows that right always wins and that wrong always loses.

Her garments of strength and honor protect her from the foul winds of popularity which blow so many women over the precipice of worldliness and disgrace.

"But she that liveth in pleasure is dead while she liveth."—I Tim. 5:6.

"A good name is rather to be chosen than great riches, and loving favour rather than silver and gold."—Prov. 22:1.

PRUDENT

"She openeth her mouth with wisdom; and in her tongue is the law of kindness."—Prov. 31:26.

To be prudent is to be "practically wise, careful of the consequences of measures or actions; judicious; cautious; circumspect."

You would expect this woman to give good advice. She can be firm and yet very kind. People like to confide in her because she never gossips. Everyone knows that she is truthful and values her friendship. She cannot be numbered among the people described in the following poem:

PEOPLE WILL TALK

Yes, people will talk; the saying is true.
They talk about me; they talk about you.
If we go to the opera, someone will say,
We should go to church and learn how to pray.

If we go to church and offer up prayers,
They say we are hypocrites and putting on airs.
If we are rich, they call us a thief,
Scoff at our sorrows and laugh at our grief.

If we are poor, they say that we shirk,
We're always lazy, and never would work.
They talk of our prospects; they talk of our past;
And if we are happy, they say it can't last.

They talk of our loved ones; they talk of our foes;
They talk of our follies; they talk of our woes;
They talk of our joys; they talk of our fears;
They talk of our smiles; they talk of our tears;

They talk if we're single; they talk if we're wed;
They talk of us living; they talk of us dead.
Tho' we live like an angel with circumspect walk,
Our efforts are useless, for people will talk.

The reputation of many has been ruined to the gossiper's tune of, "They say!" A good policy to follow is this: know that gossip is true before you repeat it, and then don't repeat it!

"And the tongue is a fire, a world of iniquity: so is the tongue among our members, that it defileth the whole body, and setteth on fire the course of nature; and it is set on fire of hell."—Jas. 3:6.

"If any of you lack wisdom, let him ask of God, that giveth to all men liberally, and upbraideth not; and it shall be given him."—Jas. 1:5.

LOVABLE

"Her children arise up, and call her blessed; her husband also, and he praiseth her. Many daughters have done virtuously, but thou excellest them all."—Prov. 31:28, 29.

Everyone loves her because she is so lovable. She lives consistent as a mother and wife. It is natural for her children and husband to love, honor, respect and praise her.

As a true mother, she tells her children at the proper time about some facts and secrets of life which unfortunately are withheld from some. She warns them of evil, thereby making it easier for them to be overcomers. She is so tactful that they feel free to ask her questions and to confide in her. To be lovely we must love Christ and others.

"Thou shalt love the Lord thy God with all thy heart, and with all thy soul, and with all thy strength, and with all thy mind; and thy neighbor as thyself."—Luke 10:27.

GOD-FEARING

"Favour is deceitful, and beauty is vain: but a woman that feareth the Lord, she shall be praised."—Prov. 31:30.

God's ideal woman has a true perspective of values. She knows that it is easy to be deceived by favor or popularity and that beauty can be so vain and shallow.

This woman in Proverbs did not know about

Calvary and grace as we do, though I have applied the message to our day; but she was true to her God. This was the secret of her spotless character, her abiding influence and her marvelous success.

Hers was a reverential fear, which means that she stood in awe, venerated, worshiped and loved her Lord with all her heart.

Are the following verses a reality in your life?

"But seek ye first the kingdom of God, and his righteousness; and all these things shall be added unto you."— Matt. 6:33.

"That in all things he might have the preeminence."— Col. 1:18.

"For to me to live is Christ, and to die is gain."—Phil. 1:21.

REWARDED

"Give her of the fruit of her hands; and let her own works praise her in the gates."

"She shall rejoice in time to come."—Prov. 31:31, 25.

She is rewarded here and hereafter. What greater reward could she desire in this life than the consciousness that she had done her best for her Saviour, family, friends and neighbors? She was assured that her influence would never die.

What greater reward could she ask, after leaving this world, than the happy privilege of living and reigning throughout the ceaseless ages of eternity with her Saviour, the Lord Jesus Christ? She will enjoy the beautiful City, the fellowship with dear ones, the heavenly music and many other things; but the joy and thrill of the ages will be to see Jesus and to be like Him forevermore.

"Beloved, now are we the sons of God, and it doth not yet appear what we shall be: but we know that, when he shall appear, we shall be like him; for we shall see him as he is."—I John 3:2.

AN INTERVIEW WITH MY MOTHER-IN-LAW

Mrs. Nellie Kline has lived with us for 20 years and has been a great blessing to Helen and me and a wonderful spiritual help in raising our children, Carolyn and David. She is called "Nana" by the children, and most of her relatives and close friends call her "Nana Kline." She will be 90 years old on August 29, 1967, and I thought that our readers would enjoy this short interview:

"Nana, where were you born and raised?"

"In Bedford, Michigan."

"When and where did you find the assurance of salvation?"

"In a children's meeting when I was eleven years old. Later in 1918 there was a fuller assurance and consecration."

"What about your high school and college education?"

"I am a graduate of the Battle Creek High School and the University of Michigan."

"How long did you teach school, and what did you teach, and where?"

"One year in fifth grade in Battle Creek between high school and college; two years in Dowagiac, Michigan. History and English in high school, and three years English in Kankakee, Illinois high school, where I met my husband."

"How many relatives of yours or your husband's joined the teaching profession?"

"Eleven."

"What about your family, children, grandchildren and great-grandchildren?"

"My husband was head of the Mathematics Department in Louisville, Kentucky, Manual Training High School. He died in 1929. I have two children, Helen and Elizabeth; four grandchildren, and now have four great-grandchildren."

"I know that you taught Sunday school and Bible classes over the years. What did you especially enjoy teaching?"

"After the beginning of World War I, when my eyes were opened to the fact of its being a fulfillment of Bible prophecy, I think I have most enjoyed prophetic teaching."

"To what do you attribute your long life?"

"It may be due to heredity or to the longevity promise of Psalm 91:16: 'With long life will I satisfy him, and shew him my salvation.'"

"Which is your favorite verse or portion of Scripture?"

"Romans 8:28–30; Psalm 91."

"What is your favorite song?"

" 'All the Way My Saviour Leads Me.' "

"What advice do you have for young people?"

"In this 'present evil world,' there is no safety for young people outside of Jesus Christ."

"Give a few suggestions to newlyweds."

"Both should be born-again Christians. Establish a family altar and live consistent lives. Teach the children early to love Jesus."

"What advice would you give to our senior citizens?"

"For true happiness, know the Lord. One of the joys of my old age is anticipating Heaven."

"What effect does your belief in the Lord's return have on your life?"

" 'And every man that hath this hope in him purifieth himself, even as he is pure.' "—I John 3:3.

"Any suggestions concerning reading the Bible and other good books?"

"I read a chapter a day, often more, but not so much that I have to hurry, for I like to meditate on what I read. Reading other good books has been invaluable to me."

"In your opinion, who is a successful person?"

"A successful person is one who trusts Christ and follows Him all his life."

*For a complete list of available books,
write to:*
Sword of the Lord Publishers
P. O. Box 1099
Murfreesboro, Tennessee 37133.

(800) 251-4100
(615) 893-6700
FAX (615) 848-6943
www.swordofthelord.com